My Personal Touch

My Personal Touch

Mary (Duffy) Hayward

NIMBUS
PUBLISHING

Copyright © Mary Duffy Hayward, 1995, 2009

All rights reserved. No part of this book may be reproduced, stored in a retrieval system or transmitted in any form or by any means without the prior written permission from the publisher, or, in the case of photocopying or other reprographic copying, permission from Access Copyright, 1 Yonge Street, Suite 1900, Toronto, Ontario M5E 1E5.

Nimbus Publishing Limited
PO Box 9166
Halifax, NS   B3K 5M8
(902) 455-4286
www.nimbus.ns.ca

Printed and bound in Canada

Cover design: Heather Bryan

Library and Archives Canada Cataloguing in Publication
Hayward, Mary, 1919-
My personal touch / Mary Duffy Hayward.
Includes index. ISBN 978-1-55109-741-1

1. Cookery. I. Title.

TX715.6.H39 2009   641.5   C2009-901895-0

First published in 1995 by Lancelot Press, reprinted in 1997 by Nimbus Publishing (ISBN: 0-88999-598-2)

We acknowledge the financial support of the Government of Canada through the Book Publishing Industry Development Program (BPIDP) and the Canada Council, and of the Province of Nova Scotia through the Department of Tourism, Culture and Heritage for our publishing activities.

Table of Contents

Breads *13*

Cakes *37*

Buns *49*

Sweets *57*

Helpful Hints *77*

Pies *83*

Muffins *93*

Puddings *101*

Main and Side Dishes *111*

Bits and Pieces *131*

Candy *137*

Pickles and Relishes *145*

Preface

This cookbook is basically concentrated on beginners for baking and cooking. I have laid out each recipe in a very simple format based on first and second steps, etc. I know that when you get into a routine of baking breads and cookies, each step will come to you more often.

Most of my recipes are very easy and straightforward and have originated from my mother; some have been exchanged with close relatives and friends.

Just remember, successful baking takes a lot of practice and maybe along the way you will find the little helpful hints will come in handy.

To my children, I believe I brought without objection from any quarter, a dowry which contained among other things an unconscious commitment to the old saying "waste not, want not."

To my readers I hope you will learn a little something by reading it.

Mary (Duffy) Hayward

Acknowledgement

To my daughter Lynda who shared unlimited hours with me; for her patience and diligent efforts in making *My Personal Touch* a reality.

Dedication

Out of love for my eight children: Mary, Jim, John, Margie, Lynda, Tony, Debbie and Paula and their children, I dedicate this book to them.

Recipe for a Long Life

Eat half as much,
Sleep twice as much,
Drink three times as much,
Laugh four times as much.

Francis Gay
The Friendship Book, 1992

Mary Hayward

Autobiography

On April 20, 1919 in St. John's, Newfoundland I was born. My mother had three children; I was the youngest. Through the sisters of Mercy at Our Lady of Mercy School on Military Road, I received my education.

In 1930 during the great depression, my father died at the age of 43. At the age of 11, this grief, along with poor economic conditions, created a world of unending hardship, both for my widowed mother, my brother and sister.

No matter how difficult our situation progressed, my mother always managed to make ends meet. Even though there was no weekly income, she managed to put the monetary remains into her talent—baking. Our household became an instant hive of busy bakers. Mom put us all to work baking breads, cakes, cookies, wedding cakes, etc. She also prepared hot dinners and served them to customers in our dining room.

Through my mother's endurance and determination we were able to generate a survival living but most of all, to continue our education.

So from my mother, to my marriage to a fine young baker, James Hayward, I was able to raise a wonderful family of nine children and maintain through the years an enjoyment of baking.

When my children pursued a career and life of their own, my husband Jim passed away. This left me to think that I should resort to what I really enjoyed doing, baking.

Presently, I teach home baking in my residence. Pupils have ranged from all ages and they are always enthusiastic and happy with the results.

Achieving

Don't say "That's too hard to do."
Just say "I'll achieve."
Don't say "I don't understand."
Just say "I believe."

Anne Kreer

Breads

••••

"Baking Bread for Beginners"

White Bread

First Step:
In a small bowl add the following ingredients:

1 pkg.	yeast
2 tsp.	sugar
8 oz.	warm water

Let rise to surface (about 10 minutes) until well-like form appears on top of mixture; put aside.

Second Step:
In a large mixing bowl combine the following ingredients except the warm water:

5 cups	Robin Hood flour
2 tsp.	sugar
1 1/2 tsp.	salt
2 tsp.	lard, margarine or shortening

Note: 10-11 oz of warm water will be added during the second step.

Except for the warm water, rub all second step ingredients together and form a well-like shape in centre. Then add 8 oz. warm water, still working in the centre; work with right hand fingers only. Then add yeast mixture. Still working in centre, take a little flour from the sides of the bowl, add 2 oz. of warm water and again take some flour from the sides until all your flour is blended together (pretend you are making a large ball). It's going to take a little while to get it sorted out, relax but keep kneading. If at this time the dough is too tight add another ounce of warm water until a mixture is formed into a nice tidy ball.

Step 1

Step 2

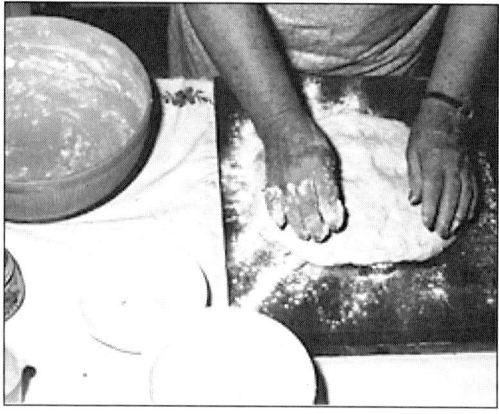

Step 3

Third Step:
Now take your ball of dough, put it on a floured board and knead the dough well. Clean your mixing bowl and grease sides with a little margarine. Place dough back into greased bowl, cover with a dry small cloth and let rise for about one hour or when dough is double in size. Make sure the room temperature is reasonably warm.

Step 4

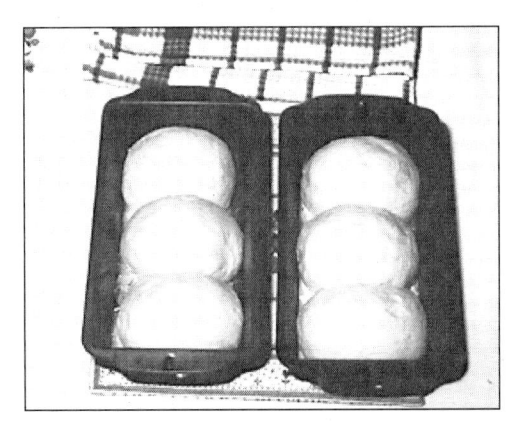

Step 5

Step 6

16 • MY PERSONAL TOUCH

Fourth Step:
Divide risen dough in six round even balls, put three balls of dough in one (1) greased pan and the remainder in the second pan and let rise again for about 1 hour or more. When oven is ready (375°F) bake your bread for 30-45 minutes until nice and brown. When baked, brush top of bread with a little melted margarine for a nice shiny appearance.

You should be proud of yourself!!!! (that's if you have followed the recipe). You have just completed baking two (2) loaves of white bread.

To make four (4) loaves of bread, double the recipe.

Please remember if room temperature is cold, it will take the dough a little longer to rise. Just keep your dough in a warm place whenever making bread.

Whole Wheat Bread

First Step:
In a small bowl add the following ingredients:

1 pkg.	yeast
2 tsp.	sugar
8 oz.	warm water

Let rise to surface (about 10 minutes) until well-like form appears on top of mixture. Put aside.

Second Step:
In a large bowl combine the following ingredients except warm water:

3 cups	Robin Hood white flour
3 cups	Robin Hood whole wheat flour
1 tbsp.	lard, margarine or shortening
3 tsp.	sugar (white or brown)
1 1/2 tsp.	salt
11-12 oz.	warm water

Except for the water, combine second step ingredients together and form a little well-like shape in centre. Add 8 oz. of warm water and keep working in centre. Work with right hand fingers only. Then add yeast mixture, still working in centre. Take a little flour from the sides of bowl and add another 3 oz. of warm water until mixture is nice and mushy. Continue to take flour from the sides of the bowl slowly and proceed until all ingredients are blended well together; knead until nice and tidy.

Third Step:
Now take your ball of dough, put it on a floured board and knead it well. Clean your large bowl and grease sides with a little margarine. Place dough back into greased bowl, cover and let rise for about one hour or when double in size.

Fourth Step:
Divide risen dough in six (6) round balls (even). Put three balls of dough in one (1) greased pan and the remainder in the second pan, let rise again for about 1 hour or more. When oven is ready (375°F) bake your bread for 30-45 minutes until nice and brown. When baked, brush top of bread with a little melted margarine for a nice golden appearance.

Bran Bread

First Step:
In a small bowl add the following ingredients:

1 pkg.	yeast
2 tsp.	sugar
8 oz.	warm water

Let rise to surface (about 10 minutes) until well-like form appears on top of mixture; put aside.

Second Step:
In a large bowl combine the following ingredients except warm water:

3 cups	Robin Hood white flour
1 cup	Robin Hood whole wheat flour
1 cup	natural bran
1 tbsp.	lard, margarine or shortening
3 tsp.	sugar (white or brown)
1 1/2 tsp.	salt
11-12 oz.	warm water

Except for the water, combine second step ingredients together and form a little well-like shape in centre. Add 8 oz. of warm water. Keep working in centre. Work with right hand fingers only, then add yeast mixture still working in centre. Take a little flour from the sides of bowl; add another 3 oz. of warm water until your mixture is nice and mushy. Continue to take flour from the sides of the bowl slowly and proceed until all ingredients are blended well together. This process will take a little time. Relax but keep kneading until your dough is nice and tidy.

Third Step:
Now take your ball of dough, put it on a floured board and knead dough well. Clean out your large bowl and grease sides with a little margarine. Place dough back into greased bowl, cover with a dry cloth and let rise for about one hour or when double in size.

Fourth Step:
Divide risen dough in six round balls (even); put three balls of dough in one (1) greased pan and the remainder in the second pan, let rise again for about 1 hour or more. When oven is ready (375°F) bake your bread for 30-45 minutes until nice and brown. When baked, brush top of bread with a little melted margarine for that appealing look.

Just remember it's always nicer when cold. If this didn't turn out right this time, it will be the next. Don't get discouraged.

Molasses Raisin Bread

First Step:

In a small bowl add the following ingredients:

2 pkg.	yeast
2 tsp.	sugar
8 oz.	warm water

Let rise to surface (about 10 minutes) until well-like form appears on top of mixture; put aside.

Second Step:

In a large mixing bowl add the following ingredients **except the water**:

5 cups	Robin Hood flour
1 1/4 tsp.	salt
2 tsp.	lard, margarine or shortening
1/3 cup	sugar
1/3 cup	molasses
1/3 tsp.	cinnamon
1 1/2 cups	raisins
11 oz.	very warm water

Except for the water combine second step ingredients together and form a little well-like shape in centre. Add 8 oz. of warm water, keep working in centre. Work with right hand fingers only. Then add yeast mixture still working in centre. Take a little flour from the sides of bowl. Add another 2 oz. of warm water until your mixture is nice and mushy. Continue to take flour from the sides of the bowl slowly and proceed until all ingredients are blended well together; knead until nice and tidy.

Third Step:

Place dough on floured board and knead well; clean large bowl and grease the sides. Place your tidy dough in the bowl and cover with a dry cloth; let rise for 1 to 2 hours until double in bulk.

Fourth Step:

Divide risen dough in six (6) even size balls. Place three (3) dough balls into one (1) greased pan and the remainder in the second pan, and let rise again until double in size. When baked, brush bread on top with a little melted margarine. It's much nicer to eat when cold.

Note: The reason I suggest two pkg. of yeast to be used is because the texture will be a lot heavier and slower to rise due to the molasses and raisins.

Christmas Bread

First Step:

In a small bowl add the following ingredients:

2 pkg.	yeast
2 tsp.	sugar
8 oz.	warm water

Let rise to surface (about 10 minutes) until well-like form appears on top of mixture; put aside.

Second Step:

In a large mixing bowl add the following ingredients **except water:**

5 cups	Robin Hood flour
1 1/4 tsp.	salt
2 tsp.	lard, margarine or shortening
1/3 cup	sugar
1/2 cup	mixed fruit
1/4 cup	cherries chopped
1 tsp.	mixed spice
1 tsp.	cinnamon
1 1/2 cups	raisins
11 oz.	very warm water

Except for the water, combine second step ingredients together and form a little well-like shape in centre. Add 8 oz. of warm water, keep working in centre. Work with right hand fingers only. Then add yeast mixture still working in centre. Take a little flour from the sides of bowl; add another 2 oz. of warm water until your mixture is nice and mushy.

Because of the added fruit this mixture will take longer to organize. Continue to take flour from the sides of bowl slowly and proceed until all ingredients are blended well together; knead until dough is formed nice and tidy. You may need to add a little more worm water if mixture is too tight.

Third Step:

Place dough on floured board and knead well: clean large bowl and grease the sides. Place your tidy dough in the bowl and cover with a dry cloth; let rise for 1 to 2 hours until double in bulk.

Fourth Step:

Divide risen dough in six (6) even size balls; place three (3) dough balls into one (1) greased pan and the remainder in the second pan, and let rise again until double in size. Bake at 350°F for about 45 minutes or less. When baked, brush bread on top with a little melted margarine.

Note: Do not let dough get cold; keep warm at all times.

One of my pupils, happy with her baking results.

Dinner Rolls

First Step:

In a small bowl add the following incredients:

1 pkg.	yeast
8 oz.	warm water
2 tsp.	sugar

Let stand until well-like form appears on top of mixture (approximately 10 minutes).

Second Step:

4 cups	Robin Hood flour
1 tsp.	salt
2 tsp.	shortening or margarine
3 tsp.	sugar
1	egg
6 oz.	warm water
2 oz.	Carnation milk 2% heated

Except for the warm water, mix together in a large mixing bowl the second step ingredients and form a well-like shape in centre. Then add warm water and milk, still working in the centre; work with right hand fingers only. Add yeast mixture, still working in centre. Gradually take a little flour from the sides of the bowl until all your flour is blended together. Keep kneading until your dough is nice and tidy.

Third Step:

Now take your ball of dough, place it on a floured board and knead it well. Clean out your large bowl and grease sides with a little margarine; place dough back into greased bowl, cover with a dry cloth and let rise for about one hour or until double in size.

Remember what I had stated earlier about a warm room temperature; your dough will take a long time to rise if the heat is not in your kitchen.

Fourth Step:
Divide risen dough in 24 little even balls and place balls together in greased pan (size should be 9 x 12). Let rise to double in size. With oven temperature at 400°F bake for 20 minutes until golden brown; brush with a little melted margarine.

Whole Wheat Dinner Rolls

First Step:
In a small bowl add the following ingredients:

1 pkg.	yeast
8 oz.	warm water
2 tsp.	sugar

Let stand until well-like form appears on top of mixture (approximately 10 minutes).

Second Step:

2 cups	white Robin Hood flour
2 cups	whole wheat Robin Hood flour
1 tsp.	salt
2 tsp.	shortening or margarine
3 tsp.	sugar
1	egg
6 oz.	warm water
2 oz.	warm Carnation milk

Except for the warm water, mix together in a large mixing bowl the second step ingredients and form a well-like shape in centre. Then add 8 oz. warm water, still working in the centre. Work with right hand fingers only. Then add yeast mixture, still working in centre. Gradually take a little flour from the sides of the bowl until all your flour is blended together; keep kneading until your dough is nice and tidy.

Third Step:
Remove your ball of dough from bowl, place it on a floured board and knead it well. Clean out your large bowl and grease sides with a little margarine; place dough back into greased bowl, cover with a dry cloth and let rise for about one hour or when double in size.

Fourth Step:
Divide risen dough into 24 little even balls and place balls together in greased pan (size should be 9 x 12). Let rise to double in size. With oven temperature at 400°F bake for 20 minutes until golden brown; brush with a little melted butter.

I know it's tempting to eat one now, but it's always better to wait!

Toutons

Put 1 yeast in to soak as if in bread.

3 cups	Robin Hood flour
3/4 tsp.	salt
1 tsp.	margarine
1 tsp.	sugar

Try 1/2 cup warm water and make well as if in bread. Add yeast and mix together, nice and tidy. Put to rise.

When risen, shape into as many little round balls as you can get, like an egg. Let rise for 20 minutes.

Pan fry them. Make sure the fat is hot. These can be deep fried as well. If you have too much dough, freeze and use later.

Toutons were one of my children's favorite treats.

Pineapple Nut Bread

2 1/2 cups	Robin Hood flour
3/4 cup	sugar
3 tsp.	baking powder
1/2 tsp.	baking soda
1 cup	bran
3/4 cup	walnuts
1	egg (beaten)
1 1/2 cups	crushed pineapple plus juice
1 tbsp.	melted margarine

First Step:

In a large mixing bowl mix flour, sugar, baking powder, baking soda and salt. Add bran and walnuts; combine beaten egg, pineapple and margarine.

Second Step:

Pour mixture into greased pan and bake for 60 to 70 minutes at 350°F. If you prefer you can place the mixture in two small pans and bake about 40-50 minutes until nice and brown.

Date Bread

First Step:

In a medium size mixing bowl, add 1 tsp. baking soda to 8 oz. of boiling water. Let dissolve, pour over dates and let cool.

Second Step:

1	egg
1 cup	brown sugar
1 cup	chopped nuts
1 tsp.	vanilla
1/2 tsp.	salt
1 1/2 cups	Robin Hood Flour
1 tbsp.	melted margarine

In another bowl beat egg and gradually add brown sugar, beating continuously after each ingredient. Add to cooled date mixture and mix well.

Stir in chopped nuts, vanilla, salt and flour; add melted margarine and mix well. Pour mixture into greased loaf pan; let stand for 15 minutes on table before baking, then bake at 350°F for 50 to 60 minutes.

Apricot Bread

2 cups	Robin Hood flour
3 tsp.	baking powder
1 tsp.	salt
1 cup	sugar
1/2 cup	chopped walnuts
1 cup	chopped dried apricots
2	eggs well-beaten
2 tbsp.	vegetable oil
1 cup	Carnation 2% milk

First Step:

In a large bowl combine flour, baking powder and salt together; add sugar, nuts and apricots and mix well.

Combine well-beaten eggs, milk and vegetable oil and add to flour mixture; mix just until all ingredients are blended.

Second Step:

Pour batter into a greased loaf pan and let stand for about 10 minutes. Bake at 350°F for 50 to 60 minutes.

Orange Nut Loaf

1 3/4 cups	Robin Hood flour
1 1/2 tsp.	baking powder
1 tsp.	salt
1/4 cup	margarine
3/4 cup	white sugar
2	eggs
2 tsp.	orange rind
1/2 cup	chopped walnuts
1/2 cup	Carnation milk 2%

First Step:

In a large mixing bowl stir flour, baking powder and salt together. Cream margarine; add sugar gradually, beating between ingredients.

Beat in eggs, one at a time, then add orange rind. Add dry ingredients alternately with milk, mixing well after each addition; fold in nuts.

Second Step:

Pour into a greased loaf pan. Bake in oven 350°F for 50-60 minutes.

Note: for this recipe I use a glaze.

2 tsp.	orange juice
1 tsp.	sugar

Let baked loaf cool for about 10 minutes. Mix orange juice and sugar together for the glaze and spread on loaf with a small brush; return to oven for about 1-2 minutes. Let cool about 15 minutes before removing from the loaf pan.

This is really tasty!

Banana Nut Loaf

1 1/2 cups	Robin Hood flour
2 tsp.	baking powder
1/4 tsp.	baking soda
1 tsp.	salt
1/4 cup	white sugar
1/2 cup	chopped walnuts
2	eggs (beaten)
1/3 cup	corn syrup
1 cup	mashed ripe banana

First Step:
Combine dry ingredients together in a large mixing bowl; add nuts and keep stirring. Make a well-like shape in the centre of the dry ingredients.

Second Step:
In another bowl mix remaining ingredients together, then pour this mixture into the well-like shape of dry ingredients and stir only until flour is moistened.

Spoon in greased loaf pan and bake at 350°F for about 60 minutes.

Words of Wisdom

The future lies before you,
Like a field of driven snow.
Be careful how you tread it,
For every step will show.

Francis Gay
The Friendship Book, 1993

Cakes
• • • •
"For Beginners"

Cherry Cake

First Step:

In large mixing bowl add the following ingredients:

3/4 cup	margarine
1 3/4 cups	sugar
3	eggs
1/2 tsp.	salt
2 tsp.	almond flavouring

Beat well until nice and creamy, then add:

1 cup	warm Carnation milk 2%
3 cups	Robin Hood flour plus 1/2 cup which goes over cherries
1 1/2 tsp.	baking powder
3 cups	cherries cut in pieces

Cream well and fold in floured cherries.

Second Step:

Grease angel food cake pan or tube pan and bake at 300°F for 1 1/2 hours. Make sure the oven has reached the right temperature. When cooked leave in pan until cold, and when cooled turn over on cake rack.

Peach Fruit Cake

1 cup	butter
1 1/2 cups	sugar
3	eggs well beaten
1 large tin	peaches crushed and well drained (save juice)
3 cups	raisins
1 1/2 cups	cherries (cut in pieces)
1 cup	coconut
3 cups	Robin Hood flour
1 tsp.	baking powder
1/2 tsp.	salt
2 tsp.	vanilla flavouring

First Step:

In a large mixing bowl cream butter and sugar. Add well beaten egg and blend in peaches, raisins, cherries and coconut. Stir in dry ingredients, add vanilla; you can add a little juice from the peaches if your mixture is dry.

Second Step:

Pour into a large greased cake pan and bake at 275°F for 3 hours.

Apricot Cake

First Step:

In a medium size saucepan, add the following ingredients:

1 3/4 cups	apricots (cut up in small pieces)
1/4 cup	sugar
1/2 cup	yellow raisins
2 cups	water

Bring mixture to a boil then let simmer for 20 minutes; cool and set aside.

Second Step:

In a large mixing bowl add:

1 cup	margarine
1 1/4 cups	sugar
8 oz.	Philadelphia cream cheese

Cream margarine, cheese, sugar then add:

4	eggs, one at a time

Blend in:

2 1/2 cups	Robin Hood flour
1 1/2 tsp.	baking powder
1 1/2 tsp.	vanilla

Fold in apricot mixture.

Third Step:

Place in greased cake pan and bake 325°F for 1 1/2 hours.

Helpful tip: place a small tin of water in oven for moisture while baking.

Rhubarb Cake

First Step:

In a medium size bowl put 1 1/2 cups of chopped rhubarb, cover with boiling water and let stand for 5 minutes.

Second Step:

In a large mixing bowl add:

1/4 cup	margarine
3/4 cup	white sugar

Cream margarine and sugar; add:

1	egg

Beat well and add the following dry ingredients:

3/4 tsp.	baking powder
1/4 tsp.	salt
1 1/2 cups	Robin Hood flour
1/4 tsp.	baking soda

Keep mixture blending and add alternately

1/2 cup	Carnation milk 2%

Fold in rhubarb mixture and add 1/2 cup chopped walnuts.

Third Step:

Pour mixture into greased pan and bake 40 minutes at 350°F. You can serve this hot or cold.

Boiled Cake

First Step:

In a large saucepan add the following ingredients:

18 oz.	cold water
9 oz.	sugar
2 tsp.	gravy browning
1 tsp.	salt
1/4 lb.	margarine
12 oz.	raisins
8 oz.	currants

Bring to a boil for 5 minutes then let mixture cool and remain in saucepan until really cold.

Second Step:

Add cold mixture to large bowl and add the following:

1 cup	chopped dates
1 cup	chopped cherries
1 cup	mixed fruit
3 cups	Robin Hood flour
1 1/2 tsp.	baking soda
1 1/2 tsp.	mixed spice
1 tsp.	cinnamon

Stir well and bake in greased pan at 275°F for 2 hours. When baked leave in pan at least 1/2 hour, remove from pan and place on a rack for further cooling.

Notes:
- You can add more fruit if desired.
- When cake mixture is in pan to bake, dip hand in cold water and smooth top of cake mixture. This will give a very smooth surface when baked.

P.S. This boiled cake recipe was passed on from my late husband Jim. We added some special touches.

Date Cake

First Step:

In a medium size bowl add:

1/2 lb.	dates (or 1 cup)
1 cup	boiling water

Set aside.

Second Step:

1/2 cup	shortening
1 cup	sugar
1 tsp.	vanilla
1 1/2 cups	Robin Hood flour
1 tsp.	baking soda
1/4 tsp.	salt

In a large mixing bowl combine all ingredients and blend them well. Add date mixture and mix well; pour mixture into greased pan, then bake at 350°F for about 30 minutes. Let cool for 1/2 hour. This can be served hot or cold.

This is nice served with cream.

Moirs Cake

First Step:

In a large mixing bowl add the following ingredients:

1/2 lb.	margarine
1 3/4 cup	sugar
3	eggs
1 tsp.	vanilla flavouring
1 tsp.	lemon flavouring

Cream well and then add the following:

1 cup	warm Carnation 2% milk
3 cups	Robin Hood flour (add flour a little at a time)
1 tsp.	baking powder

Make sure you add the flour 1 cup at a time, stirring well between cups; fold in the following:

1/2 cup	cherries (chopped)
12 oz.	raisins
1/2 cup	Robin Hood flour
	(add to fruit before folding in batter)

Second Step:

Pour batter in greased tube pan and bake at 300°F for 1 1/2 hours.

Carrot-Pineapple Cake

3 cups	Robin Hood flour
1 cup	crushed pineapple
2 cups	sugar
3	eggs, well beaten
2 tsp.	cinnamon
1 1/2 cups	Crisco oil
1 1/2 tsp.	baking soda
2 tsp.	vanilla
1 1/2 cups	chopped nuts
1 tsp.	baking powder
2 cups	raw carrot (grated and loosely packed)

First Step:

In a large mixing bowl combine all dry ingredients together.

Second Step:

Drain pineapple juice and add it to dry mixture. Add eggs, vanilla and oil, then stir in pineapple, nuts and carrots; make sure mixture has a good texture.

Third Step:

Bake in greased floured pan at 325°F for 1 1/2 hours or until your cake springs back. Leave cake in pan to cool for 10-15 minutes.

Fourth Step: Cream Cheese Frosting

In a small mixing bowl beat together:

6 oz.	cream cheese
4 tbsp.	margarine
2 tsp.	vanilla

Gradually add:

3 cups	icing sugar

Beat until smooth.

Blueberry Cake

1/2 cup	margarine
1/2 cup	Carnation milk 2%
1 tsp.	vanilla
2 tsp.	baking powder
1 cup	white sugar
2	eggs
2 cups	fresh blueberries
2 cups	Robin Hood flour

First Step:

In a large mixing bowl cream margarine and sugar, then add eggs and vanilla. Add dry ingredients, then mix well with milk. Gently fold in slightly-floured blueberries.

Second Step:

Preheat oven to 350°F. Pour mixture into a loaf pan or square pan, then place in oven and bake for about for 30 minutes.

I usually serve this recipe with a scoop of vanilla ice cream; it's really tasty!!

The Best Christmas Cake of All

1 cup of butter of faith *(to make life run smoothly)*
1 cup of sugar *(life needs its sweetness)*
5 eggs to make it light *(this is prayer, which uplifts)*
1/2 lb. of nuts *(human)*
1/4 lb. cherries *(colours the cake like music on a dull morning)*
1 lb. raisins *(are old friends, always a delight)*
1 lb. currants *(are new friends, always interesting)*
1/4 tsp. of cinnamon *(ambition)*
2 tsp. of baking powder *(to make it rise)*
1/2 cup of pure fresh whole milk *(the perfect food which is the word of God)*
1/2 tsp. of salt *(called wisdom)*
3 cups of Robin Hood flour

First Step:
Mix all well together and bake in the slow oven of experience. When well done, allow to cool.

Second Step:
Add frosting to surround it with beauty. Add red candles to light for all to see.

Third Step:
Then slice the cake and share it with others.

Morning Thoughts

Seek a fresh goal every day,
Look on all things new;

Show a smile along the way,
Let happiness shine through.

Don't give up when your plans fail,
Make another start;

Keep a trust if hope is frail;
And faith within the heart.

Set aside a time to care
And then you'll find it's true,

A kindness passed around to share
Will be returned to you.

Elizabeth Gazney

BUNS
• • • •
"For Beginners"

Tea Buns

1 1/2 cups	Robin Hood flour
1/4 lb.	margarine
3 tsp.	baking powder
2 tsp.	sugar
1	egg
1/4 tsp.	salt
1/2 cup	cold water

First Step:
In a large mixing bowl mix all dry ingredients together. Rub in margarine, add egg and water; if mixture appears too sticky, you can add a little more flour. Be careful not too much flour; stir all together until mixture becomes nice for rolling on floured board.

Second Step:
Spread mixture on floured board until 3/4" thick, then with a sharp bun cutter cut out your buns and place on greased cookie sheet. Brush with a little Carnation milk and let rise for about 20 minutes. Turn oven on to 400°F and bake for about 10 to 15 minutes until nice and brown.

These buns go over really well and they're one of Lynda's favourites!!

Step 1

Step 2

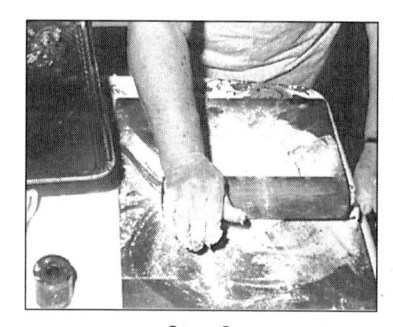

Step 3

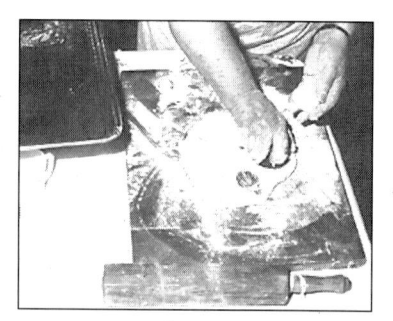

Step 4

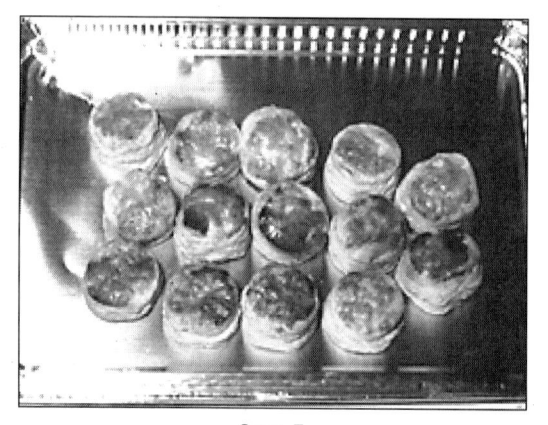

Step 5

BUNS • 51

Raisin Buns

1 cup	Robin Hood flour
3 oz.	margarine
2 1/2 tsp.	baking powder
1/3 cup	sugar
1/4 tsp.	salt
1 cup	raisins
1	egg
1/2 cup	cold water

First Step:
In a large mixing bowl add dry ingredients and rub all together until blended. Add egg and water until it forms a ball of dough.

Second Step:
Roll dough on floured board until 3/4" high. Cut out buns with a sharp bun cutter and place on greased cooking sheet; brush with Carnation milk and let rise for 20 minutes. Turn oven on to 400°F; bake for 10 to 15 minutes until nice and brown.

P.S. It's got to be a sharp bun cutter.

Cheese Buns

1 cup	Robin Hood flour
2 1/2 tsp.	baking powder
1/2 cup	grated cheese
1 tsp.	sugar
3 oz.	margarine
1/4 tsp.	salt
1/4 to 1/2 cup	cold water

First Step:
In a large mixing bowl rub dry ingredients together until nice and crumbly. Add egg and 1/4 or 1/2 cup water; roll out on floured board (until about 3/4").

Second Step:
Cut out with a sharp bun cutter; place on greased pan and brush with Carnation milk. Place some grated cheese on each bun and bake at 400°F until golden brown.

Nicer served hot!! Try them.

Mary is very fond of these buns!!

Cinnamon Buns

First Step:
In a small bowl add the following ingredients:

1 pkg.	yeast
2 tsp.	sugar
8 oz.	warm water

Let rise to surface (about 10 minutes) until well-like form appears on top of mixture; put aside.

Second Step:
In a large mixing bowl add the following dry ingredients:

4 cups	Robin Hood flour
1/4 cup	sugar
1 tsp.	salt

Mix all dry ingredients together then add:

1 cup	warm Carnation milk 2%
1	egg
2 tbsp.	margarine or shortening, melted

Form a nice soft dough. Add yeast mixture and keep kneading until dough is nice and tidy. Remove dough from bowl; clean bowl and grease it. Place dough back in the greased bowl and let rise until double in bulk.

Third Step:
Place risen dough on floured board and roll till about 1/2" in thickness; brush with 1/4 cup melted margarine.

Fourth Step:
Combine 1/2 cup sugar, 2 tsp. cinnamon, 1/3 cup raisins, then sprinkle this mixture over the dough and roll up like a jelly roll. Cut in 1" slices and place on greased cooking sheet approximately 10" x 15". Separate each roll by 1" apart; let rise again until double in bulk. Bake at 375°F for about 25 minutes. You need two (2) cooking sheets.

Fifth Step:
In a small mixing bowl add 1 cup icing sugar, 1 tbsp. boiling water and 1/2 tsp. vanilla flavouring; apply over baked buns.

This recipe appears to have a lot to it, but once you try it's very simple. This was a favourite for all my children.

These buns were Margie's favourite treat after school!!

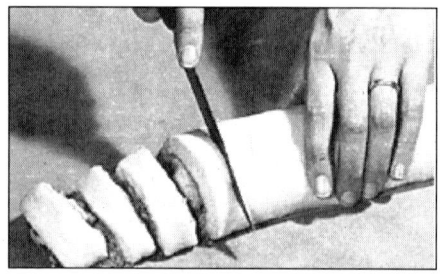

You can also form a ring, as shown.

Here's a poem with a sense of humour for those of us who are getting "so called younger." It reads:

When people's cars get old and worn
and they begin to toddle
They go somewhere and trade them in
And get the latest model.

Now I have very often thought
That when my joints get achy
And when my hair has all turned grey
And knees are very shaky.

And when the onward march of time
Has left me rather feeble
How nice t'would be to find a firm
That deals in worn-out people.

And when my form is bent with age
And gets to look shoddy
How nice it would be to turn it in
And get a brand new body!

Francis Gay
The Friendship Book, 1993

SWEETS
····

Caramel Squares

First Step:
Preheat oven to 350°F.

Second Step:
Cream thoroughly the following ingredients:

1/2 cup	margarine
1/2 cup	lightly packed brown sugar

Add:

1	beaten egg yolk and blend well.

Add:

1 1/4 cups	Robin Hood flour

Combine thoroughly. Spread this mixture over bottom of a greased 8" square pan.

Third Step: Topping
In a small mixing bowl beat 1 egg white to stiff peaks then blend in 1 cup lightly packed brown sugar, 1 tsp. vanilla, 1/8 tsp. salt and 1 cup chopped nuts. Spread mixture over batter in pan. Bake for about 30 minutes until golden brown.

Special Note: Brown sugar is very moist and therefore extra care should be taken when measuring it in order to use the right amount. When measuring with a cup the best way is to pack it firmly into the cup so that the sugar just holds the cup shape when turned out.

Lemon Squares

First Step:

    1 pkg.   lemon filling

Mix as directed on package; use only 1 1/2 cups boiling water. Let cool.

Second Step:

1 cup	Robin Hood flour
1 cup	coconut
1 cup	plain biscuit crumbs
1 cup	white sugar
1 cup	margarine (about 1/2 lb.)

In a medium size mixing bowl combine ingredients together to form a crumbly mixture. In a greased square pan place 1/2 of crumb mixture on bottom; pour cool lemon filling on top of mixture, then add remainder of crumb mixture and press down with a fork to even off.

Third Step:

Preheat oven to 350°F. Bake for about 1/2 hour or less, then cut into squares when cooled.

Partridgeberry Squares

1 cup	partridgeberries
1/2 cup	margarine
1 cup	brown sugar
1 1/2 cups	Robin Hood flour
1 cup	coconut
2	egg yolks, well beaten
1 tsp.	baking powder
1 tsp.	vanilla

First Step:
Cream margarine and sugar, and add egg yolks and vanilla. Add flour and baking powder, bake for 15-20 minutes at 350°F.

Second Step:
Remove from oven and add 1 layer of partridgeberries.

Third Step:
Into beaten egg whites add 1 cup brown sugar, stir and place mixture over partridgeberries. Sprinkle 1 cup coconut, then return to oven and bake at 350°F until golden brown.

Date Squares

First Step: Filling
In a medium saucepan put the following ingredients:

1 cup	dates
3/4 cup	cold water
1 tsp.	sugar

Place over medium heat until mixture is boiled and soft; mash and let cool, then set aside.

Second Step:

1 cup	brown sugar
1 cup	Robin Hood flour
2 cups	rolled oats
8 oz.	margarine
1/4 tsp.	salt
1/4 tsp.	baking soda
1/4 tsp.	baking powder
1/4 cup	coconut

In a large mixing bowl crumble all ingredients and place one half of this mixture in a greased 8 x 10 inch pan. Spread date filling over pan mixture, then spread remaining crumbled ingredients over date filling and sprinkle coconut over final topping.

Third Step:
Bake for 30 minutes at 350°F. When baked let cool and cut into squares.

Peanut Butter Cookies

First Step:

1/2 cup	soft margarine
1/2 cup	brown sugar
1/2 cup	white sugar
1/2 cup	creamy peanut butter
1	egg
1 tsp.	vanilla

Cream mixture 2 minutes with electric mixer at medium speed.

Second Step:

1 cup	Robin Hood flour
1/2 tsp.	salt
1 tsp.	cinnamon
1/2 tsp.	soda

In a large mixing bowl add flour, salt, cinnamon, and baking soda. To this mixture add the first step mixture and blend slowly scraping bowl often. Drop on greased cookie sheet, flatten with fork and bake at 350°F for 12 minutes. This recipe makes about 2 1/2 dozen cookies.

Chocolate Chip Cookies

1 cup	Robin Hood flour
1/2 tsp.	salt
1/2 tsp.	baking soda
1/2 cup	chocolate chips
1/2 cup	chopped walnuts
1/2 cup	margarine
2/3 cup	brown sugar

First Step:

In a large mixing bowl stir in the first three ingredients; mix 2 tablespoons of dry ingredients with the chocolate chips and walnuts and set aside.

Second Step:

Cream margarine and add brown sugar gradually, beating until very creamy. Beat in

1	egg
1/2 tsp.	vanilla

Add dry ingredients, mixing well; fold in the chocolate chips and nuts.

Third Step:

Drop mixture by teaspoonfuls onto greased cookie sheet and bake at 375°F for 8 to 10 minutes or until done. Cool before removing from cookie sheet.

Oatmeal Cookies

2 cups	Robin Hood flour
1 tsp.	baking soda
1 tsp.	salt
2 cups	rolled oats
1 cup	brown sugar
1/2 cup	margarine
1/2 cup	shortening
1/2 cup	sour milk
	(2% Carnation milk with 1 tsp. white vinegar)

First Step:
In a large mixing bowl stir the first 5 ingredients together.

Second Step:
Melt margarine and shortening and mix with dry ingredients. Stir in sour milk and mix well. Chill dough 1/2 hour then roll out about 1/4" thick on lightly floured board. Cut with round cookie cutter to about 2 inches in diameter.

Third Step:
Place on a greased baking sheet and bake in oven at 350°F for 10 to 15 minutes or until lightly browned.

This recipe makes about 4 dozen.

Shortbread Cookies

1/2 cup	cornstarch
1/2 cup	icing sugar
1 cup	Robin Hood flour
3/4 cup	margarine

First Step:

Stir cornstarch, icing sugar and flour together. Blend in margarine with spoon, mixing until a soft smooth dough forms.

Second Step:

Shape dough into 1 inch balls and place about 1 1/2 inches apart on an ungreased cookie sheet. Flatten with a lightly floured fork. If dough is too soft to handle, cover and chill for about 1 hour.

Third Step:

Bake in oven at 300°F for 20 to 25 minutes or until edges are lightly browned.

This makes about 3 dozen cookies.

Coconut Crisps

2 cups	Robin Hood flour
3/4 tsp.	baking powder
1/4 tsp.	salt
3/4 cup	margarine, softened
1 cup	sugar
1	large egg
1 tsp.	vanilla flavouring
1 cup	coconut

First Step:
Preheat oven to 375°F.

Second Step:
In a large mixing bowl combine flour, baking powder and salt.

Third Step:
In a mixer bowl beat margarine and sugar at medium speed until light and fluffy. Beat in egg and vanilla. With mixer at low speed, beat in dry ingredients just until combined. Stir in coconut.

Fourth Step:
Drop dough by level tablespoonfuls onto ungreased cookie sheets. With bottom of glass dipped in flour, flatten each cookie to 1/4" thickness, then press with back of fork to form ridges. Bake 10-12 minutes, until edges are golden brown. Makes 2 1/2 to 3 dozen.

Oatmeal-Raisin Cookies

1 cup	Robin Hood flour
2 tsp.	baking soda
3/4 tsp.	salt
1/4 tsp.	nutmeg
1/2 cup	margarine softened
1 cup	firmly packed brown sugar
1/2 cup	white sugar
1 tsp.	vanilla flavouring
2	large eggs
3 cups	rolled oats, uncooked
1 1/2 cups	raisins

First Step:

Preheat oven to 350°F. Grease two (2) cookie sheets and set aside.

Second Step:

In a large mixing bowl combine flour, baking soda, salt and nutmeg.

Third Step:

In a mixer, beat butter and sugars at medium speed until light and fluffy. Stir in vanilla. Add eggs one at a time, beating well after each addition. With mixer at low speed, beat in flour mixture just until combined. Stir in oats and raisins.

Fourth Step:

Drop dough by heaping tablespoonfuls 2 inches apart onto prepared cookie sheets. Bake 12 to 14 minutes until golden. Cool on cookie sheets 1 minute, then transfer to wire racks to cool. This makes about 2 1/2 dozen.

Spicy Drop Cookies

1/2 cup	margarine
1/2 cup	sugar
1	egg
1/2 cup	molasses
2 cups	Robin Hood flour
1 tsp.	ginger
1/2 tsp.	nutmeg
1/2 tsp.	cloves
1/4 tsp.	salt
1 tsp.	baking soda dissolved in 1/2 cup hot water
1/2 cup	raisins

First Step:

In a mixer, cream margarine and sugar. Add egg and molasses. Combine flour, salt and spices. Add gradually with the hot soda water. Fold in raisins or other chopped fruit such as dried apricots, apple or maybe chocolate chips.

Second Step:

Drop from teaspoon onto lightly greased cookie sheets. Bake in 350°F oven for 10-15 minutes. This makes about 3 dozen cookies.

Chocolate Snow Balls

First Step:

In a medium size saucepan *boil* for 3-4 minutes,

1/4 cup	margarine
1/2 cup	Carnation milk
2 cups	white sugar

Add:

2 tbsp.	cocoa

Second Step:

Let cool a little, then add:

2 cups	coconut
2 cups	rolled oats
1 tbsp.	vanilla

Third Step:

Roll mixture in balls and then roll in coconut on waxed paper; place in refrigerator and let cool. There's no cooking needed.

Makes about 2 1/2 dozen.

The kids will really love this treat.

Coconut Macaroons

1 cup	white sugar
2	egg whites
2 tbsp.	cornstarch
2 tbsp.	boiling water
1/2 tsp.	vanilla

First Step:

Place all ingredients in double boiler and keep over the boiling water. Beat mixture until peaks form. Remove from heat and thicken with coconut.

Second Step:

Drop by level tablespoonfuls onto greased cookie sheet. Bake at 350°F.

Makes about 1 dozen cookies.

Two-Carrot Diamonds

2	eggs
1 cup	brown sugar
2/3 cup	cooking oil
1 3/4 cups	Robin Hood flour
1 tsp.	baking powder
1 tsp.	ginger
1 cup	shredded carrots (2 or 3 medium size carrots)
3/4 cup	raisins

First Step:

In a medium size mixing bowl combine eggs, brown sugar and cooking oil; beat until well mixed together. Add flour, baking powder, ginger, 1/4 tsp. salt and beat until a smooth mixture is formed. Stir in carrots and raisins.

Second Step:

Prepare oven to 350°F. Pour batter into baking pan (regular size) and bake for 20 to 25 minutes. When baked remove from oven and cool, and cut into diamonds. Store in fridge.

Third Step:

Spread cookies with cream cheese icing prepared as follows:

In a small mixing bowl beat together:

3 oz.	cream cheese
2 tbsp.	margarine
1 tsp.	vanilla

gradually add:

2 cups	icing sugar

beating until smooth.

Hermits

1 cup	raisins, washed and dried
1 cup	chopped dates
1/2 cup	chopped mixed fruit
1/2 cup	chopped nuts
1/2 cup	soft margarine
1/2 cup	soft shortening
1 1/2 cups	brown sugar
1/3 cup	honey
1 tsp.	vanilla
3	medium eggs, beaten
2 cups	Robin Hood flour
1 tsp.	baking powder
1/2 tsp.	baking soda
1/2 tsp.	salt
1 tsp.	cinnamon
1/2 tsp.	nutmeg
1/4 tsp.	cloves
1/2 cup	whole wheat Robin Hood flour

First Step:
Prepare fruits and nuts.

Second Step:
In a large mixing bowl cream butter and shortening together, add brown sugar gradually. Beat well; add honey, vanilla and beaten eggs. Combine thoroughly. Add dry ingredients and stir in the whole wheat flour and fruits and nuts. Chill mixture for one hour.

Third Step:
Drop by heaping teaspoonfuls onto greased cookie sheets and bake in moderate oven at 375°F for 8 to 10 minutes. When baked cool on rack. This makes 4 to 5 dozen cookies.

Brownies

1 1/2 squares	unsweetened chocolate
3 tbsp.	butter or margarine
1 cup	white sugar
1/2 cup	Carnation milk
1 cup	Robin Hood flour
2 tsp.	baking powder
2	eggs, unbeaten
1/4 cup	chopped walnuts
1 tsp.	vanilla
1/4 cup	coconut (if desired)

First Step:
Melt chocolate and butter together and blend well. Set aside.

Second Step:
In large mixing bowl combine sugar, milk, flour, baking powder and unbeaten eggs. Add melted chocolate mixture. Beat vigorously until mixture is smooth and thick. Add vanilla and nuts. Pour into greased 8 x 12 inch pan and bake at 350°F for 30 to 35 minutes.

Third Step:
Immediately upon removing from oven, cut in squares. Cool slightly and lift from pan. Frost if desired with favourite chocolate frosting.

Ginger Snaps

1 cup	molasses
1 1/2 tsps.	baking soda
1/2 cup	lard
1 tsp.	ginger
1 tsp.	cloves
1 tsp.	cinnamon
3 cups	Robin Hood flour

First Step:
Boil molasses for 5 minutes. Remove from heat and add soda, lard and spice. Stir in enough flour to make a stiff dough. Let stand until cold.

Second Step:
Roll thin and cut out with cookie cutter. Bake at 375°F. Makes about 6 or 7 dozen thin, crisp cookies.

Watch them very closely while in the oven as they can burn very easily.

Ginger Snaps were one of my mother's favourites.

Be Optimistic

Don't look for faults as you go through life;
But if perhaps you find them
Remember it's wiser and kinder to turn a blind eye,
And seek for the virtues behind them.

Francis Gay
The Friendship Book, 1993

HELPFUL HINTS
••••

Play Dough

There were many hours enjoyed by my children with homemade play dough. Here's how to make it:

In a small bowl add 1/4 cup flour and 1/4 salt; add enough of water to moisten. Form a dough ball; keep moulding dough ball until nice and soft for play. Add a drop of colouring for appearance.

Place play dough in plastic bag when not in use.

Salt

Hot salt brine is good for sinks and drains; it cuts away grease and unfriendly odours.

Old Fashioned Starch

1 tbsp.	cornstarch
1/2 cup	cold water

In a small bowl add cold water to cornstarch and stir until mixture becomes thick. Once thickened add about 2 cups of boiling hot water; mix well. Touch up with a spoonful of detergent.

Wet the garment to be starched; apply starch mixture and work in well. Let semi-dry and iron.

Aspirin Gargle

2 aspirin tablets, 1/2 cup warm water; let aspirin dissolve and stir. Gargle 4 times a day; this really helps a sore throat.

No-Snarl Wool

If you are ever knitting with two balls of wool just slip the two strands of wool through a large bead. You will find the bead keeps the wool snarl-free.

Knitting Accessories

In your knitting basket keep a cosmetic bag to hold measuring tape, darning needles, etc. I find this really handy; it keeps everything in one place and ready at hand.

Dried-Out Shoe Polish
Add a couple of drops of turpentine, close the can tightly and set it aside for a few days. You'll have the shiniest shoes ever!!!

Soft Brushes
In the middle of a painting job you can sometimes be interrupted. When this happens and to avoid problems with your brushes, simply place them in a plastic bag and close the bag tightly. You will be able to resume painting later with a brush that is co-operative; the brush will be soft as when you first started. Follow this procedure with paint rollers too.

Hard to Clean?
Slip a sock over your hand for those hard-to-get-at places. Your hand is more flexible than a rigid brush.

Easy Drip-Dry
For your drip-dry sweaters one of the last things you should do is hang them on the clothesline with clothes pegs. At the very least you can expect unsightly distortion. Try this: roll up a towel of suitable length and slip it through the sleeves. Then peg the towel to the clothesline.

Thinner Nail Polish
When your nail polish starts to thicken just add a drop of vegetable oil.

Sewing Buttons
Next time one of your buttons come off your blouse or shirt, sew it with dental floss. It will keep it there for a long time.

Dry Tobacco
To guard against dry tobacco (for cigarette or pipe), add a small piece of potato to your tobacco pouch.

Cleaning Walls and Windows

Take a pail of warm water and add a quarter cup of household bleach and a splash of white vinegar; your walls and windows will become bright and clean. I have found out through experience to wash from the bottom up. There'll be no streaks, and no rinsing will be needed.

Sparkling Sinks

Usually after a while you will notice your kitchen sink becoming dull or just plain tired looking. You can whiten it easily by just adding a little bleach to a sinkful of warm water; leave it for a couple of minutes, then you will see a difference. For tougher stains add a little more bleach.

Carpet Wear

To protect areas of carpet some people, myself included, have put down large squares of leftover carpeting thinking it would save wear and tear. In reality, the coarse backing of the added carpet works like sandpaper on the carpet underneath, making it wear even more.

Try Not To Worry

Worry is like a rocking chair
It doesn't get you anywhere!

Put your feet down on the ground,
Walk about, and look around.

Don't just sit there — up and do;
Don't let worry, worry you.

Life goes on!

Carole Glade

PIES
••••

Pastry

2 cups	Robin Hood flour
1/3 tsp.	salt
1/2 cup	shortening
1/3 cup	butter
1/3 cup	ice cold water (approximately)

First Step:

Combine flour and salt into a bowl. Cut in shortening and butter with two knives. Stir in ice cold water a little at a time until mixture forms a ball that cleans the bowl. Cut dough into two balls.

Second Step:

With as little handling as possible, form into a flat surface and place on a lightly floured board. Roll out lightly in two directions away from you and towards you to form a large oval.

Third Step:

Fit loosely into two pie plates, pressing lightly but firmly into bottom and sides. Trim the edge and flute, or let pastry overhang the edge by 1/2 inch. Fold under and crimp attractively. Prick bottom and sides in several places if shells are to be baked before filling.

Just remember the less pastry is handled, the better quality texture!!!

An Easy Apple Pie

1 cup	Robin Hood flour
2 tsp.	white sugar
1	egg
1/4 lb.	margarine
2-4	apples
1 tbsp.	cinnamon
2 tbsp.	brown sugar

First Step:

In mixing bowl rub dry ingredients together until crumbs are formed; add egg and 2 tbsp. ice cold water or a little more if needed. Mis with fork until you form a nice ball. Cut dough in two parts. Roll out very thin on floured board one part of dough to cover a regular size cookie sheet.

Second Step:

In small mixing bowl add 2 tbsp. brown sugar, 1 tbsp. cinnamon and stir. Sprinkle this mixture over the rolled dough. Cut very thin slices of apple; cover the mixture of brown sugar with apple mixture and repeat again. Cover with second part of dough rolled out as the first. Prick top of dough with knife; brush with Carnation milk. Let stand for 15 minutes and bake at moderate oven (400°F) until golden brown.

Fresh Cream Pie

1 cup	white sugar
1 cup	raisins
1 cup	sour cream
1 tsp.	Robin Hood flour
1/2 tsp.	cinnamon
1	egg beaten

Mix the first five ingredients together. Add beaten egg. Cook in double boiler till thick. Remove from stove. Add 1 tsp. baking soda. Spread in a baked pie shell. Chill. Cover with whipped cream.

Lemon Meringue Pie

First Step:

In a medium size saucepan mix the following ingredients:

2	egg yolks (beaten)
1/3 cup	cold water
1 pkg.	lemon pie filling

Cook over medium heat, stirring constantly until filling thickens and bubbles. Remove from heat and stir in 1 tbsp. margarine. Cool 5 minutes, stirring twice.

Second Step:

Prepare pastry and follow instructions as previously mentioned.

Third Step: Meringue

2	egg whites
1/4 cup	sugar

Beat egg whites until soft peaks form. Gradually beat in sugar until stiff peaks form. Top pie with meringue. Bake at 350°F until golden brown (approximately 12 minutes). Cool before serving.

This was Tony's favourite pie when he was a young boy.

Raisin Pie

1 cup	brown sugar
2 tbsp.	Robin Hood flour
1 cup	water
	grated rind of one lemon
	juice of one lemon
2 cups	raisins
	pastry
	pinch of salt

First Step:

In top part of a double boiler combine sugar, flour and salt. Add the water, lemon rind and juice; add the raisins. Cook over hot water for 15 minutes, stirring occasionally. Let cool.

Second Step:

Meantime, line a 9-inch pie pan with pastry and prepare enough pastry for strips for top of the pie. Add cooled filling and top with pastry strips in lattice fashion. Bake at 450°F for 10 minutes, reduce heat to 350°F and bake for another 20 minutes or until pastry is done.

Fresh Blueberry Pie

First Step:
Prepare pastry as previously directed.

Second Step:

1/4 cup	Robin Hood flour
1 cup	white sugar
1/8 tsp.	salt
4 cups	fresh blueberries
1 tsp.	lemon juice
1 tbsp.	margarine

Line the pie pan with pastry. In a small bowl combine flour, sugar and salt together and sprinkle 1/4 of it over uncooked bottom crust. Add the blueberries and remaining sugar mixture. Sprinkle with lemon juice and dot with margarine. Add top crust, seal the edges and flute. Bake at 450°F for 15 minutes, then reduce heat to 350°F and continue baking until berries are tender (for about 30 minutes).

In the summertime when my son Jim was very young, he picked a lot of fresh blueberries and would request a blueberry pie in return. By the way — he still enjoys blueberry picking.

Rhubarb Pie

4 cups	rhubarb, cut in 1/2 inch pieces
1 1/2 cups	white sugar
3 tbsp.	quick-cooking tapioca
1/4 tsp.	salt
1 tbsp.	margarine
	pastry

First Step:

Prepare pastry as previously directed.

Second Step:

Combine rhubarb, sugar, tapioca and salt. Place in a pastry lined 9-inch pie pan; dot with margarine. Top with 1/2 inch wide strips of pastry to make a lattice effect. Flute edge. Bake at 450°F for 10 minutes, reduce temperature to 375°F and continue baking for another 25 minutes until rhubarb is tender.

Lassy Tart

First Step:

Prepare pastry as previously directed. Line an 8-inch pie shell and prepare pastry strips for the top.

Second Step:

Prepare the following filling:

1	egg
1 cup	molasses
1 cup	soft bread crumbs

Third Step:

Beat the egg; add molasses and beat until combined. Stir in bread crumbs.

Fourth Step:

Pour into uncooked pie shell. Top with strips of pastry and bake in a 400°F oven for approximately 20 minutes or until pastry is lightly browned and the filling is firm.

Preserved Children

1 large grass field
1/2 dozen children
2 or 3 small dogs
some pebbles
few drops of brook
a few flowers

Mix the children and the dogs together. Put them in a field, stirring constantly. Pour the brook over the pebbles, sprinkle the field with flowers.
Spread all over a deep blue sky.
Bake in the hot sunshine.
When well browned remove to the bathtub.

Francis Gay
The Friendship Book, 1992

MUFFINS
••••

Blueberry Muffins

2 cups	Robin Hood flour
3 tsp.	baking powder
1 tsp.	salt
1/2 cup	sugar
2	eggs
1 cup	Carnation milk 2%
1/4 cup	melted margarine
3/4 cup	fresh blueberries

First Step:

In a medium size bowl combine flour, baking powder, salt and sugar together.

Second Step:

In a medium size bowl, beat eggs well. Add milk and melted butter; pour this liquid mixture into dry ingredients. Stir quickly until ingredients are just mixed; fold in slightly floured fresh blueberries.

Third Step:

Grease muffin pan; pour batter into pan until pan is about 2/3 full. Bake in hot oven at 400°F for about 15 to 20 minutes.

Makes 1 dozen.

Bran Muffins

1 cup	Robin Hood flour
2 tsp.	baking powder
1/2 tsp.	baking soda
1/2 tsp.	salt
1 cup	whole bran
1/2 cup	milk
1/3 cup	molasses
1	egg
1/4 cup	shortening
1/2 cup	raisins

First Step:
In a large bowl combine flour, baking powder, baking soda and salt.

Second Step:
In another bowl combine bran, milk and molasses. Let stand until most of the moisture is taken up; add egg and shortening and beat well.

Third Step:
Add raisins to the dry ingredients. Blend into bran mixture, stirring only until combined. Fill greased muffin pans to about 2/3 full; bake in a hot oven at 400°F for about 20 minutes.

Makes 1 dozen.

Apple Muffins

2 cups	Robin Hood flour
2 tsp.	baking powder
1/4 cup	white sugar
1/2 tsp.	cinnamon
1/2 tsp.	salt
1 cup	Carnation milk 2%
1	egg, well beaten
1/4 cup	melted margarine
1 cup	finely chopped apple

First Step:

In a large mixing bowl combine dry ingredients; stir in chopped apple.

Second Step:

Combine beaten egg, milk and melted margarine; stir. Pour into flour and apple mixture; stir until dry ingredients are moistened. Spoon into lightly greased muffin pan and bake in 400°F oven for about 20 minutes.

Makes 1 dozen.

Spicy Oat Bran Muffins

1 cup	Robin Hood flour
1 cup	oat bran cereal
2 tsp.	lightly packed brown sugar
1 1/2 tsp.	baking powder
1 tsp.	cinnamon
1 tsp.	nutmeg
1 tsp.	salt
1 cup	Carnation milk 2%
2	eggs
1/4 cup	melted margarine
1 tsp.	vanilla

First Step:

In a mixing bowl, combine flour, oat bran, brown sugar, baking powder, cinnamon, nutmeg and salt; make a well-like shape in mixture.

Second Step:

In a small bowl, beat together milk, egg, margarine and vanilla and pour this mixture in well in dry ingredients. Stir quickly until lightly mixed. Do not overmix; mixture should be rough and lumpy.

Third Step:

Divide evenly into greased muffin pan, filling each 2/3 full. Bake in 400°F oven for 20 minutes or until golden brown.

Makes 1 dozen.

Peanut Butter Muffins with Banana Chunks

1	egg
1 1/2 cups	Carnation milk 2%
1/2 cup	crunchy peanut butter
1/2 cup	firmly packed brown sugar
1/4 cup	vegetable oil
1 cup	bran cereal
2	medium bananas
2 cups	Robin Hood flour
1 tbsp.	baking powder
1/4 tsp.	salt

First Step:

Grease large muffin pan and pre-heat oven to 400°F.

Second Step:

In a medium size mixing bowl beat together egg, milk, peanut butter, brown sugar and oil until well combined. Stir in cereal, let stand 5 minutes. Slice bananas lengthwise in quarters, cut crosswise into chunks and stir into cereal mixture. Mix remaining ingredients in large bowl. Stir cereal mixture into dry ingredients, stirring just until moistened. Spoon into muffin pan, generously filling each to the top. When baked cool on rack. Store in airtight container.

Makes 1 dozen.

Love

Love is something if you give it away,
You end up having more.

It's just like a magic penny,
Hold it tight and you won't have any;

Lend it, spend it, and you'll have so many,
They'll roll all over the floor.

Francis Gay
The Friendship Book, 1992

PUDDINGS
● ● ● ●

Caramel Pudding

First Step:

In a bowl put the following ingredients:

1 cup	Robin Hood flour
1 tsp.	baking powder
1	egg
1/4 cup	sugar
2 tbsp.	margarine
6 tbsp.	Carnation milk 2%
2	small apples

Combine all ingredients in a greased casserole dish.

Second Step:

Pour over mixture:

1 cup	brown sugar
1 1/4 cups	boiling water
1 tbsp.	margarine
1 tsp.	vanilla

Bake at 400°F for 35 minutes; serve hot.

Plum Pudding

2/3 cup	margarine
1 cup	molasses
1/3 cup	raisins
2 cups	Robin Hood flour
1 tsp.	cinnamon
3/4 tsp.	allspice
1/2 tsp.	nutmeg
1 tsp.	baking soda
1 cup	Carnation milk 2%

In medium size bowl, beat margarine, sugar and molasses together. Add all dry ingredients alternately with milk; steam in pudding cloth or steamer for three hours.

Lemon Sponge Pudding

3	eggs, separated
1 1/2	lemons, rind and juice
2 tbsp.	Robin Hood flour
1 cup	white sugar
1 cup	Carnation milk 2%
pinch	salt

In a medium size mixing bowl add rind and juice to egg yolks, add flour and sugar slowly. Beat well and add milk slowly. Beat egg whites stiff and fold into the mixture. Pour into a greased casserole set in a pan of water and bake 45 minutes at 325°F or until set.

Cheese Apple Crisp

1 1/4 qts.	apples, peeled and sliced
1/4 tsp.	cinnamon
3/4 cup	water (room temperature)
3/4 tbsp.	lemon juice
1 1/2 cups	white sugar
1 cup	Robin Hood flour
1/4 tsp.	salt
1/2 cup	margarine
1/2 cup	shredded cheese

First Step:

Arrange apples in a shallow baking pan, sprinkle with cinnamon. Add water and lemon juice.

Second Step:

Combine sugar, salt and flour; work in margarine to form a crumbly mixture. Lightly stir in shredded cheese. Spread this mixture over the apples and bake at 350°F until the apples are tender and the crust is golden brown and crisp.

Quick Raisin Pudding

1/4 cup	brown sugar
1 cup	Robin Hood flour
2 tsp.	baking powder
1/4 tsp.	salt
1 cup	raisins
1/2 cup	Carnation milk 2%

First Step:

Mix together in a greased casserole the sugar, flour, baking powder, salt and raisins. Stir in the milk.

Second Step:

1 cup	brown sugar
1/2 tsp.	nutmeg
1 tbsp.	margarine
2 cups	boiling water

Sprinkle sugar and nutmeg on top of batter and dot with margarine. Pour on boiling water. This forms the sauce for pudding. Bake at 375°F for 30 minutes.

Apple Pudding

First Step: Batter

1/4 cup	shortening
1/2 cup	sugar
1	egg, beaten
1/2 cup	Carnation milk 2%
1 cup	Robin Hood flour
2 tsp.	baking powder
1/4 tsp.	salt
1/2 tsp.	vanilla

Slice peeled apples into a greased baking dish, sprinkle with cinnamon or nutmeg. Cream shortening, sugar and egg together; then add milk alternately with sifted dry ingredients. Add vanilla. Spread over apples.

Second Step: Sauce

1 cup	brown sugar
1 tbsp.	margarine
1 tsp.	vanilla
1 1/2 cups	water

Combine all ingredients and boil for 5 minutes. Pour over batter and bake for 35 to 40 minutes at 350°F.

Old Fashioned Figgy Duff

3 cups	bread crumbs
1 cup	raisins
1/2 cup	brown sugar
pinch	salt
1 tsp. each	gnger, allspice and cinnamon
1/4 cup	melted margarine
3 tbsp.	molasses
1 tsp.	baking soda
1 tsp.	hot water
1/2 cup	Robin Hood flour

First Step:
Soak stale bread and crusts in water for a few minutes. Squeeze out the water and rub between the hands to make crumbs. Measure without pressing down in the cup. Combine the bread crumbs, raisins, sugar, salt and spices and mix with a fork. Add melted margarine, molasses and soda which has been dissolved in the hot water. Now add the flour and combine well.

Second Step:
Pour mixture into a dampened pudding bag; tie tightly leaving a little slackness to allow the pudding to expand. Boil for 1 1/2 hours. Serve with heated molasses.

This pudding goes well served with corned beef and cabbage dinner.

Apple Cobbler

6	apples, peeled and sliced
3/4 cup	brown sugar
1 tbsp.	margarine
1 1/2 cups	Robin Hood flour
2 tsp.	baking powder
1/4 tsp.	salt
2 tbsp.	shortening
1	egg, well beaten
6 tbsp.	Carnation milk
1/4 cup	granulated sugar
2 tbsp.	boiling water
1/2 tsp.	vanilla

First Step:
Arrange sliced apples in a greased baking dish. Sprinkle with brown sugar and dot with margarine.

Second Step:
In a medium size mixing bowl, combine flour, baking powder and salt together. Cut in the shortening. Combine well beaten egg and the milk; add to the flour mixture and mix lightly to a soft dough.

Arrange dough over the apples and pat down gently to completely cover the apples. Bake at 425°F for 15 minutes.

Third Step:
Remove from oven and lower temperature to 350°F. Pour the sugar, boiling water and vanilla mixture over the top. Return to the 350°F oven and bake for another 20 minutes.

Bakeapple Pudding

1/2 cup	margarine
1 cup	brown sugar
1 cup	Robin Hood flour
2 cups	rolled oats
1 tsp.	baking soda
1 1/2 cups	fresh bakeapples (sweetened) or
1 1/2 cups	bakeapple jam

In a mixing bowl place margarine, sugar, flour, rolled oats and baking soda. Rub with fingertips until fine and crumbly. Spread half of mixture into pie dish. Spread with bakeapples or bakeapple jam. Cover with remaining crumb mixture and gently press down with hands until even. Bake in moderate oven 350°F until golden brown.

Having Faith

If faith can move a mountain
It can move a little hill,
And your prayers will soon be answered
If you're certain that they will.

It may take weeks or months or years,
It may not take that long,
But faith can move a mountain
If that faith is good and strong.

Jean Harris

MAIN AND SIDE DISHES
••••

Fish and Brewis

First Step:

    5 cakes   hard bread

Soak hard bread in cold water for 24 hours.

Second Step:

    1 pound   salt fish
    8 strips   bacon
    2   large onions
    1 tbsp.   butter

Fry bacon and drain fat, cut bacon in small pieces. Chop 2 large onions and put in bacon pan (make sure bacon is removed). Put cover on and steam on slow heat until tender.

Boil cakes of bread for 1 minute, drain well. Cook fish until done, remove bones from fish and add to the hard bread. Add chopped onions and bacon; blend with mixture. Add lump (approx. 1 tbsp.) of butter and serve very hot.

This serves 6 people.

This is one of Debbie's favourites!!

Fish, Potatoes & Drawn Butter

1 pound	salted fish steaks
10	potatoes (average size)

First Step:
Soak fish for 24 hours in cold water, then drain.

Second Step:
Boil fish in cold water for 15 to 20 minutes and in a different saucepan boil your potatoes until done.

This meal is served very nicely with parsnips and/or your favourite vegetable, and drawn butter.

Drawn Butter

2 cups	cold water
2 tsp.	margarine
1	onion (medium) chopped
1 pinch	salt
1 pinch	pepper
1/2 cup	Carnation milk

First Step:
In a medium size saucepan cook the above ingredients over medium heat until tender. Add 1/2 cup Carnation milk; boil for a few minutes and set aside on low heat.

Second Step: Thickening

2 tbsp.	Robin Hood flour
1/4 cup	cold water

In a small bowl mix the above ingredients until very smooth. No lumps please — this mixture should be somewhat thick.

Third Step:
Add thickening to heated mixture in saucepan and let simmer over medium heat until nice and tasty. This serves four.

This is John's favourite meal!!

Moose Pot Pie

First Step:
Cut 2 pounds of moose meat into small bite-size pieces and roll in 1/2 cup Robin Hood flour and 2 tsp. salt, until the pieces are well coated. Place in oven with a little shortening or pork and brown. Then add 4 cups of water and simmer for about 2 hours.

Second Step: (in this order)

6	medium carrots, sliced
2	onions, chopped
1	small turnip, diced
3	parsnips, sliced
8	medium size potatoes, cut in small pieces

Potatoes are added last because they require less cooking.

Third Step:
Now cook for about 25 minutes or until the vegetables are just tender. Add more water if needed but keep the juice thick enough for gravy.

Cover the meat and vegetables with pastry and bake at 425°F, until pastry is ready (about 15 minutes).

Baked Flippers with Vegetables

2	flippers
3 slices	salt fat pork
2	onions
1	turnip
2	carrots
1	parsnip
5 or 6	potatoes
	salt & pepper to taste

First Step:

Remove all fat from the flippers. Wash and cut in serving pieces. Do not parboil. In bake pot fry out the salt pork; remove "scrunchions" (fat back pork). Brown flippers in this fat. Then add a little water and simmer until tender.

Second Step:

Add chopped onions and cut up vegetables, except potatoes. Season and add about 1 1/2 cups of water. Cook about 30 minutes and then add the potatoes. Cook another 15 minutes, adding a little more water, if necessary.

Third Step:

1 cup	Robin Hood flour
2 tsp.	baking powder
1/2 tsp.	salt
1/4 cup	shortening
1/2 cup	water (or less)

Prepare pastry as previously discussed. Roll pastry out to fit your bake pot. When the flippers and vegetables are cooked, cover mixture with pastry and bake at 425°F for 20 minutes or until nicely browned.

Serves 2 or 3 hearty appetites.

Potato Salad

1 cup	mayonnaise
1 tsp.	vinegar or lemon juice
1 1/2 tsp.	salt
1 tsp.	sugar
1/4 tsp.	pepper
4 cups	cooked chopped potatoes
1 cup	sliced celery
1/2 cup	chopped onion
1/3 cup	grated carrot
1	hard boiled egg, chopped

Combine the first five ingredients in a small bowl and mix well. Combine the remaining ingredients in a large bowl; add dressing and toss to make sure all ingredients are coated well. Place in refrigerator for at least two hours; this will help season all flavours.

White Sauce

4 tbsp.	Robin Hood flour
4 tbsp.	margarine
1 cup	Carnation milk 2%
1 pinch	salt
1 pinch	pepper

Over low heat melt margarine in medium size saucepan. Stir in flour, mixing very well. Add milk and stir constantly — remember to increase your heat until mixture is very smooth and thick. Add salt and pepper to taste. Just in case it's too thick, add a little hot water.

This sauce is nice served with salmon.

Also by adding 1/2 cup of grated cheese to this sauce, it makes a nice cheese sauce to serve with broccoli.

Fried Cod Heads

Four medium-sized cod heads after they have been sculped (see note below). Prepare to cook as follows:

Cut heads in two; skin and remove lips. Wash well and dry. Dip both sides of head in Robin Hood flour, sprinkle with salt and pepper to taste. Fry in fat until golden brown on both sides. Serve with potatoes and green peas, or any vegetables you prefer.

To sculp: With sharp knife, cut head of fish down through to the eyes. Grip back of head firmly and pull.

This was a favourite treat for my late husband Jim.

Scalloped Potatoes

First Step:
Peel 6 large potatoes. Slice thinly and place in a buttered 2 quart baking dish in layers. Cover each layer with a sprinkle of Robin Hood flour, dot with margarine, and season with salt and pepper.

Second Step:
Fill the dish with hot Carnation milk 2% up to the top layer of potatoes and sprinkle with grated cheese. Bake slowly until tender (about 1 1/4 hours) at 350°F.

Shepherd's Pie

First Step:

1 pound	medium ground beef
1	medium size onion
3/4 tsp.	salt
1/4 tsp.	pepper
1-10 oz.	tin timato soup
1-10 oz.	tin green peas

Chop the onion and fry with ground beef; drain excess fat. Place cooked meat and drained peas in a casserole dish and cover with whipped potatoes (see second step).

Second Step: Whipped Potatoes

5	medium potatoes, cooked
1/2 cup	Carnation milk 2%
1	egg, beaten
pinch	salt

Mash potatoes when still very hot and add other ingredients; apply as above in first step.

Place in oven at 300°F for about 20 minutes.

Savory Potatoes

4 cups	mashed potatoes
1	small onion (finely chopped)
	pepper to taste
2 tbsp.	margarine
1-2 tbsp.	savory

Add onion and pepper to mashed potato. Add margarine and savory; blend well. Press into a casserole dish; dot with margarine and brown in a 400°F oven.

Mustard Glaze for Ham

1/2 cup	brown sugar
1/2 tsp.	dry mustard
2 tbsp.	fruit juice
	whole cloves

Mix brown sugar, dry mustard and fruit juice. The last 30 minutes of cooking time, spoon fat from ham pan. Stud ham with cloves. Spoon over ham; baste occasionally.

Fish Chowder

1 pound	fresh or frozen fish fillet
2 cups	potato, peeled and chopped
1/2 cup	chopped carrot
1/2 cup	chopped celery
1/2 cup	chopped onion
1 tsp.	salt
1/2 tsp.	pepper
2 cups	Carnation milk 2%
3 tbsp.	Robin Hood flour
1/2 tsp.	thyme, crushed

First Step:

Thaw fish if frozen and cut into 2 inch squares.

Second Step:

In a large saucepan bring 2 cups of water to a boil; add potatoes, carrot and celery. Reduce heat. Cover, and let simmer for about 15 minutes. Stir in fish, onions, pepper and salt. Let simmer while covered for about another 10 minutes.

Third Step:

Combine a small amount of Carnation milk with flour to make a liquid paste; remember, no lumps. Add remaining milk, flour paste and spices to vegetable mixture. Cook and stir till bubbles appear on top.

Vegetable Pork Pie

4	pork chops
1 cup	water
3 cups	potatoes (sliced)
2 cups	turnip (sliced)
	salt and pepper to taste

First Step:
Brown pork chops in frying pan. Remove chops and drain fat from pan. Add water to pan.

Second Step:
Parboil potato and turnip in small amount of water. Place vegetables in casserole with enough water (in which they were cooked) to almost cover.

Third Step:
Add salt and pepper on top and bake in moderate oven for 30 minutes.

Fourth Step:
Remove from oven and cover with biscuit dough. To make it, just follow the following instructions:

1 cup	Robin Hood flour
2 tsp.	baking powder
4 tbsp.	shortening
1/3 tsp.	salt

Roll out 1/4" thick to fit casserole and place over chops. Bake at 450°F for 12-15 minutes.

Good Old Fashioned Stew

First Step:
Using any kind of meat you wish — moose, rabbit or beef — cut in pieces, season and brown well in frying pan.

Second Step:
After well browned, add water. Cover and let simmer for about 2 hours. Using vegetables of your choice, cut into bite size chunks and add with onions; cook until tender.

Third Step:
The last ten minutes add thickening and spoon dumplings as follows:

1 cup	Robin Hood flour
2 tsp.	margarine
2 tsp.	baking powder
1/2 tsp.	salt
1/4 cup	cold water

Combine all ingredients, mix well and let rise for about 5 minutes; spoon on stew.

Dumplings

1 cup	Robin Hood flour
2 tsp.	baking powder
1/2 tsp.	salt
1/2 cup	Carnation milk 2% or water

Stir together flour, baking powder and salt. Add in milk. Drop by spoonfuls over your favourite pea soup or stew.

Corned Beef Cakes

10	medium size potatoes, cooked
1/2 tsp.	salt

First Step:

In a large bowl place cooked potatoes and salt; add 1 tin of cooked corned beef. Trim all fat from beef. Chop beef small and add to hot potatoes.

Add the following:

1 cup	chopped onion
1 tsp.	savory
1/2 tsp.	pepper

Second Step:

Mash well and form cakes; dip in flour. Fry in pan until golden brown.

This makes about 12 medium size cakes.

Macaroni & Cheese

First Step:
In a 1/2 gallon boiling salted water add 2 cups of elbow macaroni; let boil until tender (about 15 minutes).

Second Step:
Drain and rinse with cold water and drain again. Place 1 1/2 cups of chopped cheese and 2 tbsp. Carnation milk and let simmer until cheese is melted.

For an added treat this is really tasty if you add 1 tin of hot stewed tomatoes. Also, just before serving add 1 slice of creamed cheese and let melt. Serve very hot.

This is Paula's favourite lunch.

Salmon Loaf

1 large tin	salmon (bone and flaked)
2 cups	hot cooked rice
2	eggs (beaten)
2 tbsp.	melted margarine
	juice of lemon
	salt and pepper to taste

Mix all ingredients together. Bake in covered pan set in hot water for 1 hour at 325°F. This is served nicely with tomato sauce.

Sweet & Sour Stew

First Step:

1 pound of boneless stewing meat

Cut meat in very small bite size pieces and fry in pan with a little cooking oil until brown.

Second Step:

Add the following ingredients to fried stewing meat:

2	carrots (grated)
2	onions (chopped)
1 tbsp.	Worcestershire sauce
1/2 cup	water
1/4 cup	vinegar
1/4 cup	brown sugar
1 tsp.	salt
1 tin	tomato paste (14 oz.)

Mix 1 tbsp. cornstarch to 1/4 cold water; pour into above ingredients. This is good served over rice.

Five-In-One Casserole

2	medium potatoes, sliced
2	medium onions, sliced
1 lb.	minced steak
1 cup	cooked rice
1	large can tomatoes
	salt and pepper to taste

First Step:
Grease a fairly large casserole.

Second Step:
Slice potatoes and onions rather thin. Put potatoes in bottom of casserole, then onions, cover with minced steak, then rice and finally spoon some of the tomatoes over all. Season each layer with salt and pepper. Bake in moderate oven at 350°F for 1 1/2 hours or until potatoes and onions are soft. As the dish cooks, it may be necessary to add more tomatoes.

Thrifty Supper Casserole

1/2 lb.	ground round steak (or any ground beef)
1 1/4 cups	canned tomatoes
1/2 cup	chopped onions
1 tsp.	Worcestershire sauce
pinch	salt
pinch	pepper
1 can	peas, drained
1/2 cup	buttered bread crumbs

First Step:
Brown the meat well in frying pan. Add tomatoes, onions, seasoning and simmer.

Second Step:
In a greased casserole place alternate layers of peas and meat sauce. Sprinkle with buttered bread crumbs and bake 20 minutes at 450°F.

Think of Others

Busy people always seem
The ones who understand
Someone else's problems,
And find time to lend a hand;

Yes, we all have problems
But life has often shown
By overcoming others' woes
We overcome our own.

Francis Gay
The Friendship Book, 1993

BITS AND PIECES
••••

Salt

Salt has played a major role for all baking and cooking needs. The following tips are some ways salt has other uses:

- When whipping cream, if you add a pinch of salt to the mixture it will whip more readily;
- When cooking apples a pinch of salt will make them more tender and add to the flavour;
- Boil potatoes in salt water for ten minutes before baking in oven — they bake faster;
- Cake icing will not sugar if you add a pinch of salt;
- Always wash green vegetables in salt water; any living animal life will come to the top;
- When tea is spilled on a tablecloth, cover the stain at once with salt. Leave for a little while. When cloth is washed the stain should be removed.
- Shake fine salt in your frying pan before frying fish and the fish will not stick to the pan.

Tomato Peeling

This is very tricky. Just core and freeze. The next day allow the tomato to thaw slightly, then slip off the skin.

Frozen Tomato Paste

Lots of times when cooking tomato paste some is left over. To freeze, place tomato paste portions (say tablespoon size or to your own taste) on a cookie sheet, freeze and then place in a plastic bag, like so many frozen hockey pucks.

Omelets

An ordinary cheese omelet will really leap to attention if you add a teaspoonful of prepared mustard.

Ripen Fruit

To ripen fruit or vegetables, just place them in an ordinary plastic bag, put a small hole in the bag and leave them at room temperature.

Double Duty

These days, with the accent on saving energy, your double boiler should get more use than ever. While cooking a vegetable in the lower part, you can also warm leftovers, heat soup, or steam another vegetable. I'm sure you'll find it useful for other dishes.

Tasty Chicken

Massage your chicken with olive oil, then sprinkle a little rosemary over it. Shake salt and pepper to taste; this is really nice.

Meat Slices

Many of us are probably aware of the convenient way to slice raw meat. When partially frozen it will cut easily; however your fingers will become partially frozen as well, so wear an oven mitt and slip a plastic bag over the mitt to keep it clean.

Icing Idea

When preparing frosting for cupcakes, use peanut butter instead of ordinary butter. The appearance and taste is different and super for a change.

Easing Measuring

Save yourself a lot of messy washing up when measuring solid shortening, butter, or similar ingredients, by filling a measuring cup with water less the measure required. For example, if you use 1/4 cup of butter, fill the measuring cup to the 3/4 level with water, add butter until the water rises to the one cup mark. End result, you have your quarter cup of butter and no hard-to-clean measuring cup.

Storing Fruitcake

The most important point to remember when storing your fruitcake is the cakes must be totally cooled off before you prepare them for storage. If you wrap your cakes while they are still warm, you run the risk they will become mouldy during storage — a major disappointment after going through the effort of baking a cake.

For short storage, wrap well in heavy foil and store in a cool dry place.

For long storage, dip several thickness of cheesecloth in sherry or other spirits (not table wine). Squeeze out excess and wrap the cake in the prepared cheesecloth, then in heavy duty foil and store in a cool dry place.

Recycling Fruit Tins

For a pleasant change when baking breads, save three 14 oz. fruit tins, line with wax paper and place mixture of breads in tin (banana or date, etc.).

Moose or Caribou: Tips for Cooking

Steaks: Peel off the membrane around the muscles which cause the gamey odour and taste. Then, in a heavy iron skillet over a high heat, sear both sides of the steak in light fat. Turn the heat down to medium and cook to the desired rareness.

Roasts: Marinate a roast in a beef barbeque sauce, using a covered crockery or other non-metal dish, for 24 hours. Then, pour the remaining sauce over the roast. Roast in a low oven for the same time as you would a similar weight beef roast.

Frosting Tips

A cake should always be cold before a frosting is spread over it. Frost top only, for economy.

Counting My Blessings

One day, when I was lonely,
Why, I began to count,
I thought of all my blessings,
How that total seemed to mount!

I thought of all the good times
My dear family and good friends
And the laughter and the kindness,
Yes, that total really grew!

I found it rather wonderful
I couldn't have believed
That God could be so good to me
Such love I have received.

Jean Harris

CANDY

••••

Fudge

1 2/3 cups	sugar
2/3 cup	Carnation milk (whole)
2 tbsp.	butter
1/2 tsp.	salt
2 cups	miniature marshmallows
1 1/2 cups	semi-sweet chocolate chips
1/2 cup	chopped walnuts
1 tsp.	vanilla

First Step:

In regular size saucepan combine sugar, milk, butter and salt; cook, stirring over medium heat until mixture comes to a boil. Boil 4 to 5 minutes; make sure you stir constantly so mixture does not stick to your pan. Remove from heat and continue to stir vigorously until marshmallows melt and are absorbed.

Second Step:

Pour into foil-lined 8-inch square pan and chill. Cut into squares — make sure you keep refrigerated.

Old Fashioned Bull's Eyes

1 cup	brown sugar
1 cup	molasses
2 tbsp.	lemon juice
2 tbsp.	butter

Cook all ingredients in a saucepan; do not stir while cooking until you test a few drops in cold water.

When it forms a ball, pour out on a greased platter until it cools sufficiently to handle. Grease hands and pull — manipulate until it is a nice golden brown and snappy to touch. Pull and roll in narrow strips about the size of your thumb.

Cut into one-inch pieces with scissors and arrange on a greased platter to set hard.

Homemade Fudge

2 cups	white sugar
1/2 cup	Carnation milk 2%
pinch	salt
2 tsp.	margarine
1 cup	coconut
1/4 cup	chopped walnuts or raisins
1 tsp.	vanilla flavouring

Boil on slow heat for 3-4 minutes. Take saucepan and place in a pan of cold water; stir until thickness appears on bottom. Pour into a greased pan; cool (just remember it should be cold enough to cut). Let stand. If it doesn't get hard, boil the mixture for another 2 minutes.

For chocolate fudge add 2 tbsp. cocoa to your sugar.

Add a couple of drops of food colouring for a pleasant change.

Marshmallow Fudge

4 1/2 cups	sugar
12 oz. can	Carnation milk
3	(6 oz.) packages chocolate chips
1	10 oz. package miniature marshmallows
1/2 cup	margarine
1 tsp.	vanilla
2 cups	chopped nuts

First Step:

Mix sugar and milk in a large heavy saucepan and slowly bring to a boil. Continue to boil for about 8 minutes. Remove saucepan from heat; add margarine, chocolate chips and marshmallows and mix only until the chips and marshmallows are melted.

Second Step:

The next step is to add your vanilla and nuts. Blend and spread the mixture in a large ungreased pan. Let cool and cut into bite size squares.

Toffee Apples

First Step:
Make a syrup as follows:

2 cups	brown sugar
2 tbsp.	margarine
1 tsp.	vanilla
1 tbsp.	vinegar

In a medium size saucepan, boil until brittle. Test this by placing a sample on a spoon and put in cold water. When it cracks you know it's ready.

Second Step:
Dip apples on a stick into hot syrup; drain on unglazed paper until cold. I usually roll them in coconut for a tastier treat.

The kids loved these when they were small.

Food For Thought

Don't find fault with the man who limps
Or struggles along the road
Unless you have the shoes he wears
Or stumble beneath his load.

Don't be harsh on the man that sins,
Or pelt him with words or stones,
Unless you are sure, yea, really sure
That you have no sins of your own.

Don't sneer at the man who's down today
Unless you have felt the blow
That caused his fall, or felt the pain
That only the fallen know.

You may be strong, but still the blows
That were his, if dealt to you
In the self-same way, at the same time,
Might cause you to stagger, too.

Francis Gay
The Friendship Book, 1993

PICKLES AND RELISHES
••••

Pickled Beets

Boil young beets until tender; skin them. For each quart of beets, allow 1 1/2 cups brown sugar, 1 tsp. salt, 3/4 cup vinegar and 3/4 cup water in which beets were boiled.

Heat beets in this mixture until it boils and then fill hot sterilized jars and seal them.

Mild Mustard Sauce

1	egg, slightly beaten
1/2 cup	white sugar
1/3 cup	vinegar
1 tbsp.	dry mustard

Combine these ingredients in a saucepan and cook until thick, stirring constantly. This is delicious with ham, hot dogs or hamburgers.

Cranberry Pineapple Relish

4 cups	cranberries
1 cup	crushed pineapple
1 tsp.	lemon juice
1 cup	sugar

Put cranberries in blender. Combine with other ingredients and chill before serving.

Relish with Rhubarb

2 quarts	rhubarb (chopped)
1	medium size onion (thinly chopped)
1 pint	vinegar
2 cups	white sugar
1 tbsp.	salt
1 tsp. each	cloves, allspice, cinnamon and pepper

In a medium size saucepan cook above ingredients together slowly until tender (roughly takes about 1 hour); pour into hot sterilized jars and seal.

This is one of my favourites.

Carrot and Sweet Onion Relish

2	sweet onions, chopped
2	carrots, chopped
1 tsp.	fresh rosemary, chopped
1	bay leaf
1/3 cup	vinegar
1/3 cup	water

Combine all ingredients in a medium size bowl, stir well and cover. Refrigerate overnight.

Before serving, remove bay leaf and drain liquid. Serve with your favorite dishes.

Apple and Raisin Relish

1/2 cup	raisins
1/2	orange
1 cup	finely chopped, peeled apples
1 tbsp.	lemon juice
1/2 cup	chopped nuts
2 tbsp.	honey

Put raisins and orange (cut in pieces) through the fine blade of a food chopper. Add remaining ingredients and chill overnight in the refrigerator.

This will keep for about a week and is nice to serve with a hot or cold meat.

Let Me Do It Now

I shall pass through this world but once.
Therefore any good that I can do, any kind
act that I can perform for any fellow creature,
let me do it now.

Let me not delay, or omit it
for I shall not pass this way again.

Étienne Giennet,
18th Century

Pause for a Moment

I am only one, but I am one.

I cannot do everything,
But I can do something.

What I can do, I ought to do.

And what I ought to do,
By the Grace of God I will do.

Francis Gay
The Friendship Book, 1993

Index

Apple and Raisin Relish, 148
Apple Cobbler, 108
Apple Muffins, 96
Apple Pudding, 106
Apricot Bread, 33
Apricot Cake, 40

Bakeapple Pudding, 109
Baked Flippers with Vegetables, 115
Banana Nut Loaf, 35
Bits & Pieces, 131
Blueberry Cake, 46
Blueberry Muffins, 94
Boiled Cake, 42
Bran Bread, 20
Brownies, 73
Bran Muffins, 95

Caramel Pudding, 102
Caramel Squares, 58
Carrot and Sweet Onion Relish, 148
Carrot-Pineapple Cake, 45
Cheese Apple Crisp, 104
Cheese Buns, 53
Cherry Cake, 38
Chocolate Chip Cookies, 63
Chocolate Snow Balls, 69
Christmas Bread, 24
Cinnamon Buns, 54
Coconut Crisps, 66
Coconut Macaroons, 70
Corned Beef Cakes, 124
Cranberry Pineapple Relish, 147

Date Bread, 32
Date Cake, 43
Date Squares, 61
Dinner Rolls, 26
Dumplings, 124

Easy Apple Pie, 85

Fresh Cream Pie, 86
Fresh Blueberry Pie, 89
Fish and Brewis, 112
Fish, Potatoes & Drawn Butter, 113
Fried Cod Heads, 118
Fish Chowder, 121
Five-In-One Casserole, 127
Fudge, 138

Ginger Snaps, 74
Good Old Fashioned Stew, 123

Hermits, 72
Helpful Hints, 77
Homemade Fudge, 140

Lassy Tart, 91
Lemon Meringue Pie, 87
Lemon Sponge Pudding, 103
Lemon Squares, 59

Macaroni & Cheese, 125
Marshmallow Fudge, 141
Mild Mustard Sauce, 146
Moirs Cake, 44
Molasses Raisin Bread, 22

Moose Pot Pie, 114
Mustard Glaze for Ham, 120

Oatmeal Cookies, 64
Oatmeal-Raisin Cookies, 67
Old Fashioned Bull's Eyes, 139
Old Fashioned Figgy Duff, 107
Orange Nut Loaf, 34

Partridgeberry Squares, 60
Pastry, 84
Peach Fruit Cake, 39
Peanut Butter Muffins with
    Banana Chunks, 98
Peanut Butter Squares, 62
Pickled Beets, 146
Pineapple Nut Bread, 31
Plum Pudding, 103
Potato Salad, 116

Quick Raisin Pudding, 105

Raisin Buns, 52
Raisin Pie, 88

Relish with Rhubarb, 147
Rhubarb Cake, 41
Rhubarb Pie, 90

Salmon Loaf, 125
Savory Potatoes, 120
Scalloped Potatoes, 118
Shepherd's Pie, 119
Shortbread Cookies, 65
Spicy Drop Cookies, 68
Spicy Oat Bran Muffins, 97
Sweet & Sour Stew, 126

Tea Buns, 50
Thrifty Supper Casserole, 128
Toffee Apples, 142
Toutons, 30
Two-Carrot Diamonds, 71

Vegetable Pork Pie, 122

White Bread, 14
White Sauce, 117
Whole Wheat Bread, 18